Growth

Written by **Ruth Percival**
Illustrated by **Dean Gray**

Published in 2026 by Windmill Books,
an Imprint of Rosen Publishing
2544 Clinton St.
Buffalo, NY 14224

First published in Great Britain in 2024 by Hodder & Stoughton
Copyright © Hodder & Stoughton Limited, 2024

Credits
Series Editor: Amy Pimperton
Series Designer: Peter Scoulding
Consultant: Philippa Anderson
Philippa Anderson has a business degree and is a writer
and communications consultant who advises multinationals.
She authors and contributes to business books.

Cataloging-in-Publication Data

Names: Percival, Ruth. | Grey, Dean, illustrator.
Title: Growth / Ruth Percival, illustrated by Dean Grey.
Description: Buffalo, NY : Windmill Books, 2026. | Series: Little business books | Includes glossary and index.
Identifiers: ISBN 9781725396494 (pbk.) | ISBN 9781725396500 (library bound) | ISBN 9781725396517 (ebook)
Subjects: LCSH: Self-actualization (Psychology)--Juvenile literature. | Growth--Juvenile literature. |
Success in business--Juvenile literature.
Classification: LCC BF637.S4 P478 2026 | DDC 790.1922--dc23

All rights reserved.

All facts and statistics were up to date at the time of press.

No part of this book may be reproduced in any form without permission
in writing from the publisher, except by a reviewer.

Printed in the United States of America

CPSIA Compliance Information: Batch #CSWM26
For Further Information contact Rosen Publishing at 1-800-237-9932

Contents

4	What Is Growth?
6	Make a Plan
8	Get Help from Others
10	Borrow Money
12	New Customers
14	Take Time to Grow
16	Teamwork
18	The Right Tools
20	Listen to Good Advice
22	Take Risks
24	Spend Wisely
26	Do Your Research
28	Better Together
30	Growth and You
31	Notes for Sharing This Book
32	Glossary

What Is Growth?

Growth is when something gets bigger.

Children grow as they get older. Oaks grow from small acorns into mighty trees. Savings can help money grow.

Some growth is felt rather than seen. You feel your skills grow when you practice them. You feel your confidence grow when you do something well.

WHY DOES GROWTH MATTER?

In business, growth is very important. It might mean making money, hiring people, or taking good advice.

For you, growth might be making a plan, thinking about what others need, or asking for help.

What will our animal friends find out about business growth and about themselves?

Make a Plan

Leon Lion wants to be successful in business. But Leon has one small problem. He hasn't made a plan to help his car business grow.

Leon Lion shows Milly Monkey his plan.

She is very impressed.

Making a plan can help you to focus your ideas.

Get Help from Others

Tilly Tiger designs cool shoes for herself.

But Tilly hasn't made shoes for others, yet.

She needs help to start her business.

Peter Panda gives Tilly Tiger some money. Peter will get some of the profit when customers buy Tilly's shoes.

Growth can come from asking for help.

Borrow Money

Enzo Elephant used all his money to open a toy shop.

But he needs more money to run it.

He doesn't know what to do.

Enzo Elephant spots a sign outside the bank.

Borrowing can help with growth.
But remember, you must give back what you borrow.

New Customers

Pip Penguin's ice tour is amazing. But all her penguin friends have done the tour. Pip needs new customers!

She calls Kit Kangaroo, Kiki Koala, and Chip Cheetah. But they don't want to go.

Ice tours are too cold for us!

Pip Penguin thinks hard ... She offers a free wool hat and scarf to new customers.

Now we all want to go!

Growth means thinking about what others need.

Take Time to Grow

Monkey Adventures is fun. But Milly Monkey's trees are too small to make a *really* exciting zip line adventure park.

My trees need help and time to grow.

Milly Monkey cares for her trees. Slowly, they grow bigger and taller.

Now Monkey Adventures is the best zip line adventure park around. Everyone wants to climb, swing, and zip through these trees!

Be patient. Some things take a long time to grow.

Teamwork

Bouncing here, hopping there ... Kit Kangaroo is ever so busy running her café.

Then ... disaster! Kit Kangaroo breaks her foot!

Tilly Tiger and Pip Penguin are hired – with Kit in charge, of course!

Working as a team is great for growth.

The Right Tools

Peggy Polar Bear is making snow statues for Wei Wolf's surprise birthday party. But the snow has frozen Peggy's paws!

How will I finish the job?

Peggy Polar Bear gets a shovel and a pair of warm gloves. Now she can make even more snow statues for the party!

Choose the right tools to work smarter and faster.

Listen to Good Advice

Peter Panda thinks that **all** animals must love bamboo. He tells Omar Owl that he's going to open a business called Bamboo Biscuits.

Really? Maybe I should sell something else?

Erm ... hardly any animals eat bamboo.

Peter Panda listens to Omar Owl's good advice.

Peter decides to sell pizza instead. Phew!

Listening to good advice helps you to make clever decisions.

Take Risks

Omar Owl doesn't like his boring job. But it pays him good money. His hobby is making colorful kites.

What if my hobby can grow to become my job?

Omar Owl does lots of research into making and selling kites. He knows it will be risky, but he decides to go for it!

"I quit!"

Taking a risk can feel scary, but risks are important for growth.

Spend Wisely

Selling trees from her tree farm makes Kiki Koala money. But what should she spend the money on? A fancy car? A big house? A vacation?

Kiki Koala buys and plants more trees.

Soon she will have more trees to sell in the future.

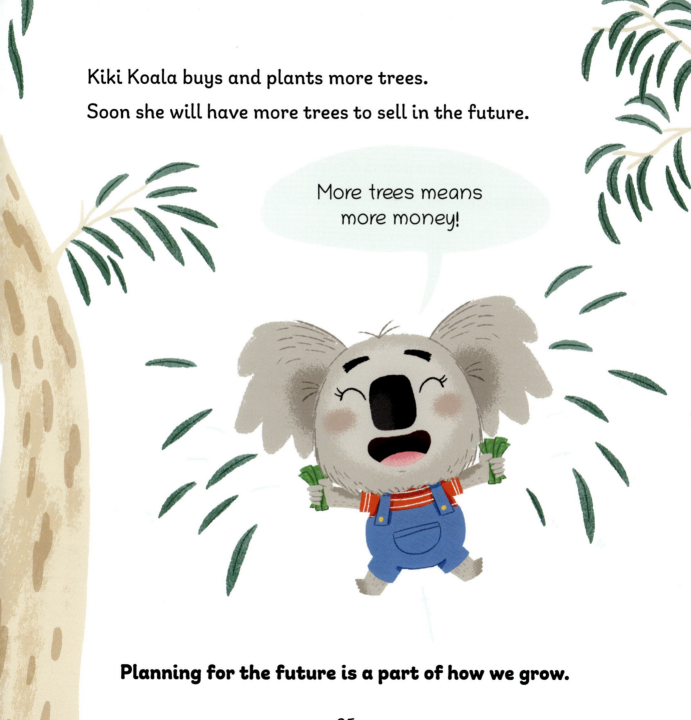

More trees means more money!

Planning for the future is a part of how we grow.

25

Do Your Research

Chip Cheetah runs yoga classes. But Tilly Tiger runs the hottest yoga class in town. Chip decides to research why it's so popular.

Chip finds out that Tilly gives her customers free drinks at every class. No wonder everyone loves Tilly's class!

Then, Chip Cheetah has a brilliant idea about how his business can compete ...

Good research can show you ways to grow.

Better Together

Wei Wolf's Hip Hats is in a great location, but he isn't selling many hats. He knows Top Caps sell lots, but their shop is small.

Wei Wolf has an idea. He makes a plan. He gets a loan from the bank and suggests they merge into one amazing shop.

Everyone thinks this is a great idea.

We'll call it Top Hats.

Joining forces can be powerful for growth.

Growth and You

Our animal friends have learned a lot about growth in business. What they have learned can help you grow, too!

Leon Lion made a plan. Try writing down or drawing your ideas to see the best way to do something.

Kit Kangaroo hired a team. As a team you can do more than when you work alone.

Omar Owl took a risk. Taking risks means trying new things, which can feel scary. Keep trying and your confidence and skills will grow.

Notes for Sharing This Book

This book introduces business ideas around the topic of growth, which link to core personal and social growth skills, such as taking good advice, teamwork, and thinking of others.

Talk to the child or class about what business is and why we need good businesses. You can use each scenario to discuss themes of growth. For example, you could talk about the child's feelings around a time they borrowed or lent a book or toy.

Growth comes from being open to new ideas and experiences. It also comes from working hard towards a goal. Talk about a time when the child tried hard at something or tried something new. How did they feel about it before and after? Did they learn any new skills?

Glossary

bank loan money lent by a bank for a set amount of time before it is paid back

business a company that buys, makes, or sells goods or services to make money

customer someone who buys goods or services from a business

focus to concentrate

hire to take on someone to work for you

hobby an interest or activity that you do for fun

merge to combine two or more things into one

profit when a business makes more money than it spends, the extra money is called profit

research to look carefully into something to see what more you can learn

risk the chance of losing something or being hurt

savings money that you keep instead of spending it. Savings are often kept in a bank